JIU
AND RESISTANCE
An Antidote to Modern Struggle

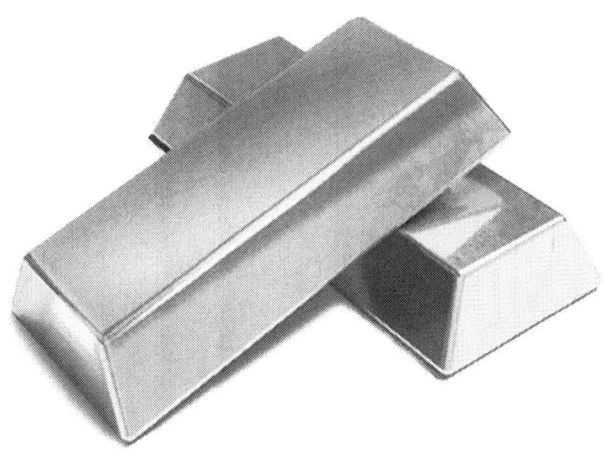

Written By
CHRIS MATAKAS

OTHER BOOKS BY CHRIS MATAKAS

My Mastery: Learning to Live Through Jiu Jitsu

My Mastery: Continued Education Through Jiu Jitsu

The Tao of Jiu Jitsu

On Jiu Jitsu

12 Rules for Jiu Jitsu

5 Rules for White Belts

Hero: The Path Through Jiu Jitsu and Life

Jiu Jitsu Kids: Roman Redefines Winning

IMPROVE: Grow As If Your Life Depends On It

The Daily Martial Artist

On Behalf of Jiu Jitsu And Wholeness

FERRYMAN PUBLISHING

FERRYMAN SERVICES, INC

FERRYMAN SERVICES, INC

28 MIRY BROOK ROAD

HAMILTON, NJ 08690

COPYRIGHT (C) 2020 BY FERRYMAN SERVICES INC

COVER DESIGN BY FERRYMAN SERVICES

EDITING BY KATHY MATAKAS

COVER ILLUSTRATION BY FERRYMAN SERVICES

ALL RIGHTS RESERVED

FIRST FERRYMAN SERVICES INC PAPERBACK EDITION MARCH 2021

FOR INFORMATION ABOUT SPECIAL DISCOUNTS FOR BULK PURCHASES,

PLEASE VISIT WWW.CHRISMATAKAS.COM

ISBN: 9798454059590

JIU JITSU AND RESISTANCE: AN ANTIDOTE TO MODERN STRUGGLE / CHRIS

MATAKAS - 1ST ED.

PRINTED IN THE UNITED STATES OF AMERICA

1 2 3 4 5 6 7 8 9 10

To my wife, Amber, who has given my life tremendous meaning, and whose heart is the compass by which we aim at the best humanity can be. Together, may we always befriend Resistance.

> *"From the beginning I had a sense of destiny, as though my life was assigned to me by fate and had to be fulfilled."*
>
> – Carl Jung

Resistance (noun): that which opposes one's intended action; the difficulty which must be encountered in the creation of anything worthwhile.

AUTHOR'S NOTE

Any work discussing Resistance must pay homage to Steven Pressfield's *The War of Art*. Like a cartographer in unknown lands, Pressfield reveals this landscape with the utmost clarity, charting the course and bringing understanding to that invisible "enemy" which we all confront. All I can hope to do with this book is offer an addendum, and just maybe, turn that enemy into a friend.

A SURPRISING DISCOVERY

I judge the merit of my academic life by the question, "What problem are you trying to solve?" The simplicity of this question has been daunting.

I began Jiu Jitsu in 2008 shortly after graduating college. Now "in the real world," I felt very much like a boy without the requisite strength to confront reality. This shortcoming was two-fold: first, I cannot escape my own insufficiencies, and second, our western culture does not provide the necessary rite of passage to turn a boy into a man.

So I manufactured that right of passage as best I could, splitting my time between the Jiu Jitsu mat and philosophy textbooks, and found my efforts surprisingly efficacious. I watched as I, along with my peers among me, slowly began to shape into an individual capable of bearing the burdens of responsibility.

Connections between the books I was reading and my experiences on the mat began to emerge. I knew of no one effectively communicating these synchronicities which I was experiencing, but they were there, ever present.

I saw how Plato's cave-dwelling man was misunderstood by those who had never seen the true sun, in the same way we are misunderstood by those who have never stepped foot on the mat. I saw how the prescriptions of the Buddha on the cessation of desires made me a better grappler, responding to the roll free of bias and taking advantage of whatever opportunities came to pass. Time and time again, I saw a deep connection between the ancient books I was studying and my training in Jiu Jitsu.

There was a golden thread connecting them which, to my knowledge, had not been articulated and as such, could not be properly understood. And therein lies the question that has driven me to write 11 books about using Jiu Jitsu as a vehicle for personal development.

"Why is Jiu Jitsu such a worthwhile tool for personal development?"

Everyone's lives improve from being on the mat. Physically, emotionally, and spiritually, we become better versions of ourselves through the crucible of training. While my friends were off winning world championships, I realized that the role I play in this community, and the role I gratefully received, is the evangelist who articulates the holistic value of our training.

But what is it that makes training Jiu Jitsu so worthwhile? How was it that our experiences on the mat were transcending into the rest of our lives, making us better people, partners, and parents? What was Jiu Jitsu *actually* doing to us?

I have spent more than a decade seeking to understand this, because you cannot remember what you do not understand. If we do not have the capacity to consciously articulate the value of a practice, we run the risk of stopping that practice and losing its benefits.

My understanding of the value of Jiu Jitsu (and the value of all disciplines) has very much followed the process of circumambulation, which we will discuss in this book. I took a roundabout and meandering approach to the conclusions I have drawn, because so much of this was confronting the unknown, stumbling forward in search of understanding.

It is with great pleasure that I now can confidently say I understand the role Jiu Jitsu plays in the life of the developing individual. There is a meta-action which is expressed in the physical, mental, and emotional benefits we enjoy, which exists in each of these domains but is supraordinate to all.

There is a deeper, more fundamental, action taking place.

The reason why Jiu Jitsu provides such holistic development, and why we can take the gains we make on the mat and apply them to the rest of our lives, is that Jiu Jitsu provides us the proper relationship to doing difficult things.

This realization is both simple and tremendously dense.

We know this. But we also don't know this, which is highlighted by the fact that so many initiates quit Jiu Jitsu before reaping all its benefits. What brings us onto the mat in the beginning is not what drives us at the end, and without a clear understanding of the purpose of our training long-term, many of us fail to possess the capacity to continue this difficult journey amid life's many responsibilities.

We owe it to each other to be better. We owe it to the Jiu Jitsu community, and the community at large, to develop the clear language that fosters understanding and keeps people on the mat long-term.

Removing the superfluous, the elevator pitch for Jiu Jitsu is simple:

Jiu Jitsu teaches us to confront Resistance in the most productive way.

When I discovered philosophy in my twenties, I waged war with the trite question, "What is the meaning of life?" Whether or not that question can be answered, embedded within is something deeper. The only reason I would ask such a question is to better understand how to act in the world. What I was really looking for when stumbling through the ancient religions and philosophies was how to use the finite time I was given.

I found that answer through the study of the archetypal hero.

Carl Jung, Joseph Campbell, and Jordan Peterson have consumed the last decade of my life for good reason. They semantically articulated how to best act in the world, codifying the role of religion and myth.

I was surprised to discover that I was learning the exact same lessons on the mat through my training. Jordan Peterson was putting words to the meta-action which was making me a better grappler and student. I realized that the greatest message the humanities had to offer was the exact behavioral process we were embodying every night in the academy, and this is precisely why Jiu Jitsu is so valuable.

Jiu Jitsu provides each of us the opportunity to daily embody the behavioral process of voluntarily pursuing the difficult on behalf of progress, and by engaging in this endeavor on the mat, we are cultivating this ability to do so in the rest of our lives.

This is paramount and is the greatest immune system against the difficulties of modern living. We must continue to train Jiu Jitsu, for the training is teaching us how to best act in the world. The remainder of this book is that lesson.

The following pages will rarely mention Jiu Jitsu and yet are deeply informed by Jiu Jitsu. We will explore the fundamental process which makes Jiu Jitsu so worthwhile to the human soul (and is the foundational precept at the root of all disciplines).

It is my sincere hope that through this amalgamation of the humanities, you will come to a clear vision of the role Jiu Jitsu plays in your life and will have cultivated the understanding of its value.

Through this understanding, may you have the strength to persevere through challenges, both on and off the mat.

VOLUNTARY EXPOSURE

There is a law of psychoanalytic theory: voluntary exposure to that which is feared is curative. The steps toward the conquering of a fear, or rather, the development of strength which is stronger than that fear, often are small. They will appear so miniscule that we can easily fail to see their value.

Imagine you are deathly afraid of snakes. The thought of being in their presence is so painful that you experience deep psychological and physiological discomfort just from producing this image in your mind.

You had a bad experience when you were a small child walking through a park. You saw a beautiful flower and ran up to pluck it. When you bent down, there was a snake coiled at its stem. Your sudden movement scared the snake. The snake's sudden movement scared you. You ran into your mother's arms, and ever since, you have had a great fear of snakes. (You haven't spent much time in parks, either.)

Imagine also, that for some strange reason which makes perfect sense in this fictional world, you are forced to become a snake handler in the local circus. Due to factors outside of your control, this is the only possible means of making money for your family, and you have no choice but to take the job.

In a heroic endeavor, you seek professional help to overcome these fears so you can support your family. You hire me as your coach with a single goal in mind: conquering your fear of snakes.

What would our action plan look like? I could go right for the jugular, and against your will throw you in a pit full of snakes reminiscent of *Raiders of the Lost Ark*. But you are not Indiana Jones, and I don't have those resources. Not to mention that with your level of anxiety, this would hardly be an effective treatment. You may become paralyzed with fear and develop PTSD, or worse, have a panic attack right there on the spot that seriously threatens your health.

This would not be wise for either of us. Exposing you involuntarily to these snakes would evoke a prey response within you. You would be the victim of circumstance. That is not restorative. We need to be more calculated and patient to achieve our intended goal.

The pathway through your fear is not obligation, it is voluntary participation.

You must engage in voluntary exposure to the degree you can manage. This would start with very small steps, but again, when it comes to the voluntary confrontation with what ails you, no step is too small. Every step is deeply significant.

We might start your first session simply talking about snakes. Toward the end of the session, after we have built up an appropriate reservoir of trust, I may challenge you (with your permission) by holding up a picture of a cartoon snake from across the room. You would be in control, and I would put it away the moment you asked. This may be only 15 seconds of our one-hour session. That's great. That's a start.

The following week, you may manage close to a minute of looking at the same picture of the cartoon snake. That's not something to sneeze at. You have quadrupled your exposure to something you find uncomfortable. If you went to the gym, and your bench press was 300% stronger than last week, you would be thrilled with your progress. This increased exposure to your fear is just as (in truth, much more) meaningful.

After that, we would graduate to a picture of an actual snake. On one hand, this form of steadily increased exposure seems silly and pathetic, which it is. But on the other hand, we are making considerable progress, and in our own way, going on a hero's journey, voluntarily pursing the difficult on behalf of the better. This is not pathetic but extremely noble. You are on a quest.

After a few weeks of looking at pictures, we could move on to watching a snake documentary on Netflix. We would watch only for a few minutes at first. You'd have the remote, and you could turn it off at any time. Maybe you only can manage watching for a few seconds. That's fine, you have moved on to voluntarily confronting something that more closely approximates that which you fear.

This is legitimate progress. The snake has not grown less scary; you have grown stronger. You are ready to continue your expansion into this fear. You're ready for the big leagues.

So we take a drive to the local pet store, a repository of snakes. I will not make you go in. I will not even ask you to get out of the car. This must be voluntary.

Upon your own volition, you summon the courage to stand outside the pet store for a few moments. This is tremendous progress!

It does not matter that the snakes are safely in their cages, inside a building with concrete walls and a shut door. For our purposes, this is sufficient exposure to threat. This may be as much as you can handle (today). That's fine. Your capacity for doing difficult things is expanding!

We return the following week, and this time you muster

the strength to open the door and stand in the doorway. Progress! You are in the process of slaying your personal dragons.

In this manner, we will continue to move along your personal continuum toward the conquering of your fears. Through this continued exposure with your fear, and through your voluntary confrontation with it, you will grow stronger. Akin to walking up a flight of stairs, every step is an irreplaceable and necessary part of the journey. No step is too small; each must be ascended to reach your goal.

With enough exposure, with enough patience and persistence, there is a high likelihood that we will reach our goal. With each successive immersion, you become stronger, and the snake less daunting. It won't be long until we get you in the store and up to the cage. Overtime, you'll continue to grow stronger, and through enough of these permutations on our central theme of being in the presence of snakes, one day you will hold one in glorious triumph.

You will then accept that job as snake handler in the local circus, becoming the hero to your family, with a deep knowledge of your capacity for progress. (You may even walk through a park to celebrate.)

This progress is remarkable, and it's not isolated just to snakes. Through this process you will have learned that you are capable of confronting difficult things and responding in a way that makes your life (and the lives of those you love) better.

You will have tapped into a reservoir of will and courage. You will have become the most recent manisfestation of the archetypal hero, voluntarily pursuing the difficult on behalf of Love.

When you look back on your training which led to this triumphant moment, you will recognize that what we had been doing all along was voluntarily confronting Resistance. This was the meta-action which was materialized in the specific action of handling a snake.

For you, the Resistance manifested itself in the form of "snake," but this is just one of countless forms that Resistance will appear in your life, and through your voluntary pursuit of the snake, you have become stronger at pursuing Resistance itself, in whatever form it may take.

When Resistance appears on the mat, in the conversations you are hesitant to have with your partner or your boss, and all those bills stacking up on your counter that you are afraid to open, you will be better suited to nobly confront these challenges. All of these are opportunities for your continued expansion. And the more you pursue them, the better your life will become. This Resistance becomes the environment which calls forth your adaptation.

I believe, through the lens of holistic development of the

individual, that this is the primary benefit we experience from our training in Jiu Jitsu. The Jiu Jitsu mat is the environment which daily provides us the opportunity to confront Resistance productively. Whether it's your first day, or your first day as a black belt, there are infinite opportunities to place yourself in a position of weakness to acquire strength. Through this consistent practice on the mats, we develop the ability to live this way in the world.

INCREASE VOLUNTARY STRUGGLE

I live by a maxim: increase voluntary struggle, decrease involuntary suffering.* To the degree that I have, my life has improved.

When I was a young boy, I played Little League baseball. Before it was my turn to go up to bat, I would take some practice swings with a donut (a weight, which looked like a donut, that slid onto the barrel of the bat). When it was my turn at the plate, I'd take the donut off, and that bat would feel lighter. I then had the increased confidence (and motor

---

* I believe I first heard this articulated from Rogan, but I cannot be sure.

recruitment) to step up the plate and give it my best shot.

I briefly fought MMA. When I did, Tuesday and Thursday mornings were our hard sparring days, during which I would spar with UFC champions. These were some of the most difficult experiences of my life, and with them came a great blessing. It did not matter what happened the rest of the day, because anything that life could throw at me would be a joy in comparison to sparring with Frankie Edgar.

I have continued to develop a practice of consistently doing difficult things which exceed the strain of my daily experience, whether intense physical exercise or intensive mental exercise like reading Carl Jung, because doing so makes the rest of my life less daunting, more accessible, and through contrast, more enjoyable.

The more difficulty I pursue voluntarily, actively seeking discomfort, the less I suffer involuntarily. The vicissitudes of life invariably become lessened, and there is the important distinction to be made: these challenges have not become less difficult; I have become stronger.

Through the voluntary exposure with the difficult, I become more capable of handling difficulty.

This is imperative in our modern world. We stand on the shoulders of the giants who came before us, reaping the benefits of thousands of years of progress. All the comforts we now enjoy shelter us from much of the natural resistance of Being. The bottom two rows of Maslow's Pyramid—food, water, warmth, shelter, and safety—are taken care of for many of us. As a result of the lack of struggle for such gifts, we have not developed the strength that such Resistance would foster.

The environment grows the organism. When our environment does not demand the cultivation of these strengths, through a conservative mechanism, the organism will not produce such abilities. As a result of our comforts, we miss out on the opportunities that such struggle creates.

Therefore, we must seek out our own Resistance, for the organism only grows in proportion to the demands of the environment. By voluntarily seeking out the difficult, we create an environment which will manifest what we can become, developing the ability to better handle the difficulties of modern life. In so doing, we do not become overwhelmed with the stresses of modern living and find ourselves perfectly fashioned to bear the burdens of being.

When we increase voluntary struggle, we decrease involuntary suffering. To the degree that we seek out such discomfort, and voluntarily engage with it, our lives will improve.

I believe Jiu Jitsu is the vehicle by which modern men and women can create the environment which produced the strength of our ancestors. Ancient life was synonymous with struggle, and therefore through causality, with tremendous endurance and strength. Jiu Jitsu serves as the rite of passage by which we return to this life of difficulty. We are given the tremendous opportunity to artificially manifest the physical struggle which our modern world fails to provide, and in so doing, tap into an ancient strength which is our birthright as humans.

THE DECISION

The most important decision I have made in my life has been my relationship to Resistance. This belief, which we will spend the remainder of this book articulating, has improved the quality of my life and the coaching clients I serve more than any other.[*]

This perspective has been a source of tremendous strength during difficult times and has provided me a framework with which I experience genuine gratitude for the Resistance I encounter. Above all, this knowledge provides

---

[*] To apply for mindset coaching with me, go to
chrismatakas.com/coaching

an endless fuel source to rise the challenges of the day.

What is this decision? To see Resistance as a gift. To understand that Resistance not only is a necessary part of life but is the pathway to life; that Resistance is the antecedent to success, and as we will discuss in the following pages, your experience of Resistance is success.

Consider yourself the hero of your own story. The hero is the one who slays the dragon on the way to the gold. The hero (you) must slay the dragon (Resistance) in the achievement of the gold (your goal). Rather than an obstacle to be avoided, the dragon is the pathway to your greatest achievement and fulfillment.

We tend to misunderstand the dragon motif. We see the dragon as an impediment to our goal, but in the practicalities of modern living, this is an inaccurate perception which creates unnecessary internal conflict. One does not have access to gold without first going through the dragon. Therefore, it is most profitable to see the dragon as an inseparable aspect of gold, something to be pursued rather than avoided.

We experience modern dragons in countless forms: sticking to a diet, paying the bills, having a necessary and difficult conversation with your partner, and all the other ways Resistance underlies our experience. Each of these encounters with Resistance offers an opportunity for expansion, for an increased quality of life, and they are ignored at our peril.

The path between your current life situation and the compelling future you envision is filled with a thick medium which opposes your movement forward: Resistance. This difficulty is a non-negotiable aspect of reality and waiting for you on the other side of these challenges is everything you've ever wanted.

You did not choose this path granted to you by birth. Thrust into experience, you have been placed on a journey that has difficulty on all sides.

To not move on the path is difficult. To move in the wrong direction is difficult. And to move in the direction most aligned with your soul (your greatest possible pathway through life) is, you guessed it, difficult.

This is a source of tremendous solace and fuel. When we understand that life is meant to be difficult regardless of one's movement along the path, suffering is transcended.

There is an interplay between opposites that governs man's existence: the natural state of things seems to be disorder, decay, and entropy, and yet man's spirit is compelled to grow and improve. In this marriage of opposites, this war between order and chaos, we are presented with the palpable tension of Resistance.

It's very difficult to create worthwhile things—businesses, marriages, homes, or yourself. The only way to create anything of value is to engage voluntarily with the forerunner of success, Resistance. Because the difficult is the change agent which propels you along the path, forcing your continued expansion into what you are destined to become.

Therefore, Resistance is the path.

This understanding is a source of strength and joy amid the countless challenges of modern living. The adoption of this belief makes one spiritually bulletproof. Everything now happens for you and not to you, and the invariable challenges of life become not only expected but welcomed.

You deserve this unshakable resolve. We're all rooting for you. When an individual becomes what he or she is destined to be, the world is better for it.

We are each cells in the organism of Humanity. Everyone plays a part; every cell has a function, and no one can play the role destined for you. Survival is not enough; you must thrive. We need what you have to offer.

We need you to pursue Resistance.

THE TIME FOR LABOR

The foundational precept which guides our working lives is wrong, and as I will demonstrate, is representative of a deeper relationship to the encounter with Resistance which must be upgraded if we are to fulfill our destiny.

We envision a distant future in which we are free from the necessity of labor, where one can finally "retire" from the strain inherent upon existence. We seem to be aiming, both tacitly and explicitly, at creating a life circumstance beyond the shackles of duty and responsibility of mere survival, in which we can just rest within ourselves, free to follow our own interests wherever they may lead.

When the sun is setting in the arc of one's life, and contentment for one's experience is the hard-won triumph of a life lived according to higher principles, the passiveness which ensues is a gift which only age and a well-lived life can grant, and should we be so fortunate to achieve that twilight, we would do well to receive this Eden with the utmost gratitude and joy in our hearts.

But for many of my readers, and most of my peers of similar age, 35, this rest is a long way off. We are now middle aged, at most. We are more like "a third aged," should we be disciplined in our health and blessed with the good fortune to ride these meat wagons until the wheels fall off.

Twilight is a far-off destination. True retirement is a foreign landmark so distant that it cannot yet be seen through a telescope. Now is no time for rest. Now is the time for action. Now is the time for labor. Now is the time for the purposeful adoption of voluntary struggle, as we are tasked with the challenge to become what we are destined to be -- that distant self which lies waiting for us in the realm of potential, longing to be made manifest with all our unique strengths and gifts.

THE IMPETUS OF TIME

When I turned 35, I experienced a profound psychological shift toward certainty. There is no more time for meandering through life away from one's purpose. It's time to get to work. And now with a clear understanding of the path, it must be walked as skillfully as possible. And there seems to be no more worthwhile skill than the discipline to continually meet the Resistance which lies between you and your destiny in a heroic, voluntary, predator-like way.

After much searching, I have found my path. I feel as though the first period of my life was spent in learning the game, and now the second period will be spent in the pursuit of its victory. God willing, a third period will be spent with loved ones in appreciation for the game itself.

But what is the trophy one hopes to attain by the end of this second period?

The achievement of becoming what one is destined to be, that deepest and truest self, which is only made manifest in proportion to the Resistance we are willing to encounter along the path.

THE CATALYST FOR GROWTH

That highest self is not object but subject. The potential we manifest is the result of being subject to an environment which demands our evolution through necessity, calling forth our maturation to survive and thrive.

Evolution is a conservative mechanism. Nothing is wasted. The law of life is simple: an organism is either growing or decaying. If an organism is not given the impetus to grow through the experience of environmental Resistance, it has no reason to spend valuable resources growing tissue which is not necessary for its survival. This is clearly demonstrated in individuals who have built up a tremendous amount of muscle mass over decades through physical training, and for various reasons, cease training and the muscle mass attained by years of hard work quickly fades.

If one's environment no longer requires great strength, then it is in the best interest of the organism to shunt that production and redistribute resources more aligned to the dictates of one's current environment.

This is an irrefutable law of nature. Therefore, we must seek out the Resistance our growth requires and continually engage in union with it.* This can all be profitably understood with a simple maxim:

The environment grows the organism.

It is the Resistance of the external world which serves as the catalyst for inner development. Our task is simply to place ourselves in the environments which will demand the adaptation our specific growth requires.

So what is the growth we require?

Growth that our soul deems valuable.

---

* I think this is why, on the whole, Jiu Jitsu academies are filled with exceptional people; we all seek the Resistance our growth requires, which is both rare and beautiful.

GROWING THE MEANINGFUL

There is a divine spark within all of us waiting to be made manifest in the world. Though we are beautiful creatures as we are, we have a deep sense that we are not in our final form, that within our genes we have still to trigger the evolution which is our birthright, to make manifest all our strengths which exist in potential, and through the voluntary pursuit of Resistance in alignment with our soul, may be made into reality, resulting in an abundance of capacity and strength to be used in the service of those with whom we interact.

I have a dear friend who has achieved tremendous professional success. He is esteemed by his community, makes a tremendous difference in the lives of those around him and has amassed great wealth. When I asked him how significant he feels his accomplishments are, he responded,

"On paper, I'm doing great." So I retorted, "But what about in your heart?" to which he admitted a deep lack of fulfillment.

He has slain dragons. He has overcome tremendous Resistance over the last decade of growing his empire. All of which were worthy and respectable triumphs, but as he so self-proclaimed, though the dragons in his wake were noteworthy, none possessed the gold he most needs. Something is missing, the Resistance which is in alignment with that faint whisper of who he knows he must become.

In order to feel that sense of self-worth and pride in his heart, on his own scorecard, which he hoped to experience through his previous successes but failed to, he must go into his heart cave and make manifest those latent aspects of his personality which lie dormant from lack of use.

We know we have more to give. We feel it, gnawing in the backs of our minds, urging us on. *"You're not done. You still have more to give. You still have more to become."* That prompting for continued action is a gift. The wisdom within us will not let us settle, because there is an intuitive genius that knows we have so much to offer humanity.

The pathway to service, to give those gifts to the world, is through the cultivation of these abilities through productive encounters with Resistance.

THE SELF: EXPLAINED

There are many ways to view the world. Each serves a purpose. All provide value. But we are limited creatures. We can only wear so many hats. Operating on the foundation of the premise that everything we do in the outer world is meant to modulate inner experience, I believe one of the most useful lenses through which to interpret our reality is psychological. It is through this lens that this book is written, and I hope to articulate my best possible answer to the aforementioned question:

What is the final goal at which our personal development aims?

The most useful (truthful) answer I have discovered comes from the works of Carl Jung. He believed what we are aiming at is the self, that experience of wholeness of becoming a fully integrated being which has merged the many aspects of the individual into one harmonious, singular form, no longer working at cross-purposes to itself, with all energies flowing in the direction most aligned with one's path.

The self is what you could be if you manifested every aspect of yourself fully, if you went through the prerequisite deaths and rebirths required to become what you are destined to be: the synthesis of your conscious and unconscious, the cultivation of your highest abilities, and the proper mitigation of your naturally inherited means towards self-destruction.

The self is what you could be if you let go of what no longer served you, and constantly oriented toward that which is of the highest meaning in accordance with your depths.

A Christ is a representation of the self. A Buddha is a representation of the self. Whom you admire, both that which you wish to possess and those who you are resentful or envious toward, possess characteristics which are aspects of the self your depths seek to manifest in the world.

The self serves many functions:

First, the self is something at which to aspire, a distant goal which beckons you forward with a promise of fulfilling one's unique purpose. The self is your north star, that distant mountain, the shiniest object you can see which compels your movement forward, through Resistance, toward what you could be.

Second, the self is a judge, for in telling you what you wish to become, it also reveals all that you are not. The self highlights your inadequacy and reveals where you are not yet enough.

And it is through these dual aspects, the presentation of a compelling future and worthy ideal coupled with the sense of inferiority and self-criticism, which will not allow you to comfortably stay as you are, that are the communication of its third and most pragmatic function: the sensation of meaning.

ON MEANING

Meaning is the empirical data that you are on your proper hero's journey moving toward the attainment of your destiny. Meaning is a tool of the self. The self provides your consciousness the experience of meaning when you are engaged in activities that will lead to its fulfillment.

Meaning is a signpost along the path of life which reads, "This Way."

Meaning comes in several forms, and part of our life's work in updating our perspective is to fashion the lens required to both see and achieve our highest goal, to develop the skill to recognize when meaning presents itself in our lives.

It would not be superfluous to differentiate between the discovery of meaning and the experience of meaning.

Meaning is found in the adoption of responsibility. Meaning is found in contribution beyond one's self. Meaning is found in the subordination of one's self to something higher, of greater value, than one's self. Meaning is found by going into the forest at the point it is darkest to you to become what you could be.

Simpler still, being that meaning is a byproduct of the fulfillment of the self, it is to be found in any endeavor that brings one closer to the achievement of that most realized being. Through the metaphor of an outward journey, meaning is found when you are on the path that leads to this final destination.

The experience of meaning, however, is entirely different and quite ironic. Meaning is found in that journey toward the self and yet is an experience of the sensation of loss of self. Meaning is experienced when we lose track of time, when we are engaged in a pursuit which our depths deem worthy. Meaning is experienced when we are deeply present, free of the sensation of being a lonely, separate "I."

Jiu Jitsu provides these experiences with repeated efficacy. The art is so demanding – both physically and mentally – that we experience that sensation of loss of self and time mid-roll.

This serves as our form of meditation, an active meditation, in which we experience so many of the benefits of eastern teachings without going to the ashram. Through our singular focus on the mats, we remove the inessential and experience a peace hard to come by in a world of endless distraction.

This absence of self and time reveals the necessity of our practice. These experiences reveal that the practice of Jiu Jitsu provides great individual meaning.

This meaning is the language of the self. The self makes things meaningful, or rather things are meaningful because their fulfillment forges us into that which we are destined to become. Meaning is the recognition from life itself that we are on the path perfectly suited for our unique nature, that we are in the process of becoming what it is our whole destiny to attain.

Pay attention to where you are pulled. When we are motivated, we push ourselves to achieve, but when we are driven by meaning, we are pulled forward. Push only lasts so long and eventually fades. Follow the pull; that is life telling you where to go.

ON MEANING, CONTINUED

How does this description of meaning enter the conversation on the meaning of life? Each man and woman must answer this age-old question for him - or herself. There are commonalities, sure, but those commonalities are the soil and roots from which we grow into unique expressions of ourselves. The meaning of life, if I could be so bold as to posit an answer, is to become what you are destined to be, to follow what most aligns with your soul, which is different for each of us.

The meaning of life is to pursue what you find meaningful.

Science tells us what is. Religion tells us how to act. But the why, that's up to you.

Though the forms change, the fundamental expression

is the same. Human beings have the innate need to grow and contribute. It is built into us. It's why we are here. The ways we grow and contribute, however, are unique to us all.

Some grow to achieve professional success. Some grow to become better partners to their spouse. Some contribute by being a master of sport. Some contribute by being a loving mother.

The modalities change, but all are vehicles leading in the same direction. The rule of the game is that we must grow. We are goal-oriented creatures, continually moving down the path toward the self, and when we don't, we suffer.

Pain is unavoidable. But the pain that has purpose, the pain that serves us on the way toward that self, is not suffering. Suffering is a result of hopelessness, of stagnation in a place we are not meant to stay and the feeling of not being able to transcend our lot in life.

And that is because to not grow, to not evolve, is to work at cross-purposes with the natural flow of life. We are meant to grow so we have more to give. The growth must serve something beyond ourselves. That's ultimately what our depths are after. This is why contribution is the final stage in the hero's journey.

The hero is only a hero because after leaving the safe confines of the known, he or she engages in some great struggle, experiencing a death and rebirth, and is reborn into someone of greater value, and it is through this heightened experience of Being that the hero shares that growth with his or her people, atoning for one's absence while on the journey through the communal distribution of the fruits acquired from that journey.

I believe each day's training session is a micro hero's journey, in which we leave home (literally, in the sense of our physical location, and psychologically, in the sense of the controlled "known" environment) and embark on an adventure into the unknown – the mat with its infinitely variable challenges which offer the opportunity for increased capability when integrated properly. It is then our responsibility to those back home, to step off the mat and bring that growth with us, with an increased capacity for service to those who made the sacrifice in our absence. If you are leaving behind a spouse and kids, this time at Jiu Jitsu is quite literally a sacrifice, and it is your efforts upon your return which determine the validity of your practice.

Every training session is a hero's journey, but the heroic process only is completed when those back home benefit from our adventure.

We learn about this heroic process through story. Whether Marvel movies, Harry Potter books, or biblical stories, these narratives convey the behavioral wisdom of how to best act in the world. That best action is almost always some variant of going on a quest and growing so we have more to give. This is what gives life ultimate meaning.

When we follow this thread, we lead to an inevitable realization.

The self is the distant goal toward which we move. The journey is one which demands our evolution to become more. This growth is the product of confronting Resistance in the most productive way, head on to strengthen our Being. In becoming more, we now have more to give, and take our rightful place in the organism of humanity, which leads us to the ultimate conclusion:

Our suffering can be transcended through the recognition that the Resistance we encounter is our greatest gift; the self pulls us forward down the path toward its attainment through the only possible medium: Resistance.

RESISTANCE AND THE PATH

Life is a journey to a distant destination. We are here and we need to venture somewhere else. We have walked physical paths, so we can use this imagery to express the path of inner development. The path is what connects two points: 1) our current position, and 2) our distant goal, a compelling future.

The only way to make that journey, to go through the process of death and rebirth in the pursuit of meaning and individuation, is to encounter the necessary Resistance along that path which will demand our evolution.

This external Resistance is a mandatory aspect of life. Our inner Resistance, however, the inner monologue we encounter which wishes the path were easy, is optional. There are no shortcuts. This is an unfolding process which takes time. When the blossom buds into a beautiful flower, using time as the vessel by which it fulfills its purpose, there is no negotiation. The development of the plant takes as long as the development of the plant requires.

In the same way, your development requires a non-negotiable amount of Resistance. These travel metaphors are fruitful. When I go on a ten-mile hike, I must hike ten miles. My philosophy, my aspirations, and the terrain and weather do not matter: to hike ten miles, one must hike ten miles.

The journey toward the self is similar. The only way to become what you could be is to experience the Resistance which will serve as the catalyst to transform you into that thing. The external Resistance is mandatory.

But the internal Resistance, the greatest source of our suffering, is optional.

TWO FORMS OF RESISTANCE: INTERNAL AND EXTERNAL

There are two forms of Resistance which we experience on the path: the Resistance which impedes our movement forward, which as we now understand, is the path toward the attainment of our goal, and the experience of internal Resistance which impedes our movement forward through a disempowering internal dialogue.

The external Resistance is non-negotiable; the internal Resistance is a habit, a thought pattern, which can be transcended. And to transcend that internal Resistance, we must address the force which shapes our lives: our beliefs.

BELIEFS

We do not so much experience the events of our lives as we experience our beliefs about the events of our lives. The same experience can happen to two different people, and they will experience two different outcomes. The same experience has happened to you multiple times in your life, and based on your state and psychology in that moment, you have responded entirely differently each time.

How is it that two people can have the same experience of losing their jobs and one responds in quiet desperation of feeling that life is against them, and it's all over, while the other interprets losing the job as a gift, a call to action to pursue a better means of employment?

The decisions we make about our experiences, what these

events mean and what we are going to do about it, shape our interpretation of events. In *Awaken the Giant Within*, Tony Robbins shares some unfortunate truths about these beliefs which govern our lives:

1. *Most of us do not consciously decide what we are going to believe.*
2. *Often our beliefs are based on the misinterpretation of past experiences.*
3. *And once we adopt a belief, we forget it's merely an interpretation.*

Until we make these beliefs conscious and choose the ones that most align with our movement forward, they will guide our lives to destinations we'd rather not go. As Carl Jung said:

"Until you make the unconscious conscious, it will direct your life and you will call it fate."

Many of us possess an internal belief that life is supposed to be easier than it is, and when we encounter Resistance which conflicts with our expectations of an experience, we reject that reality and create even more Resistance through our inner monologue.

To once again reference Tony Robbins, the master of peak performance psychology, he says that suffering is simply when reality does not match our blueprint of reality.

And when this is the case, we have two options: change the blueprint or change our reality.

There is not much we can do to change the reality of external Resistance, an irrefutable law of progress. What we can do, however, is change our blueprint. By acknowledging Resistance as an inseparable aspect of reality, we can remove the internal Resistance of wishing this were not so.

By accepting external Resistance, we transcend internal Resistance.

We can now dive in head-first and flow with the stream of life toward the final destination of who we are meant to become.

A CLEAR PATHWAY FORWARD

If our highest task is to become what only we could be, with all the unique limitations therein, then our path is clear:

1. We must first orient towards that distant self, either through intellect, intuition, or a perfect marriage of both, to have a clear goal at which to aim;

2. Once that goal is established, it is our personal obligation to our souls (and the rest of humanity) to construct the environment which will call forth our latent powers and fashion us into what we could be, to make manifest that potential, to trade "could be" for "is";

3. With the goal set, and the environment created or found, we then must walk the disciplined path of

voluntarily turning toward discomfort, pursuing the difficult, to make manifest in ourselves all that we could be.

We must struggle. We must aim up. Like a predator seeking its prey, we must hunt down the Resistance which our growth most requires, and with resolve and effort, will ourselves to victory with a singular focus.

As far as I can see it, in the struggle to preserve and prioritize one's soul amid the many dictates of modern civilization, this is the clearest pathway to fulfillment.

LONELINESS

There is a profound sense of loneliness which permeates our culture. We feel as though Huxley was right, we are "island universes," surrounded by others but ultimately playing a game of one. The world is out there, but I am in here. Nothing seems to bridge the chasm that separates the self from others.

We have become hyper-connected in this digital world, but it is a false connection: personas playing catch, throwing around attention that serves as a poor substitute for connection. We see the false highlights of others, illusory peaks which we view from our desperate troughs. We feel like the world is happening out there, and we are stuck "in here." There is a deep loneliness, a sense of being misunderstood and disconnected, which is the hallmark of the 15–35-year-olds of this age.

We are estranged, however, not from our community, but from ourselves. We have lost the ability to orient toward meaning. We got stuck playing a societal game whose prize is secondary to what we tacitly seek: a connection with ourselves.

The joy of a lifetime is to become what you are. The gift of a lifetime is to befriend your soul, to find the community within yourself, to become deeply acquainted with that spark of divinity which lies within all of us, which distraction and society dampens to a flicker, which can only be revivified through heroic endeavor.

We are lonely, because we are yet to be the hero.

THE HERO

There is unfathomable utility and profitability in studying the archetype of the hero. Immense procedural wisdom is to be uncovered in the articulation and understanding of the hero's journey, and specifically, the meta-action of the hero.

At its core, the hero's story is one of soul expansion. It is the voluntary adoption of purposeful struggle in the pursuit of the highest conceptualized good which allows for the seemingly divine acts of myth, religion, history (both collective and personal), and sport.

The hero is the one who voluntarily (though often, not at first) confronts the difficult task, shouldering the responsibility of embrace with struggle, in the acquisition of the Good (whether the receiving of a great boon or treasure, or the slaying of some great adversary), and in so doing, improves the lives of his or her people and becomes what one is destined to become (which only the proper environment [Resistance] could call forth).

The clichés are right. You are the hero of your own story, and the negation of the call is to accept one's myth as one of tragedy, a slow death in which your soul's fire dims to a flicker and ultimately becomes extinguished through atrophy. The flow of libido restricts to a slow drip; the passion of life slowly fades, and bitterness and resentment become the ghosts which haunt the once living, now dead, tomb of the soul.

The hero is the one whose soul is still alive. The hero is the one who strives for that heavenly city on the hill in the face of the Resistance which is not only the inevitable response from life, but the surefire indication that you are on the proper path: the difficulty, as Peterson said, is the destiny.

The hero is the one who forthrightly confronts Resistance. The modern hero is the one who plays detective to determine which struggle is worthy of his soul, and having found the path, puts his head down and walks it, with the smile that comes from the self-satisfaction of knowing he is playing the unique game set before him by God, of which his success is predestined.

DISTINGUISHING THE PATH FROM THE VEHICLE

So much of what we call spirituality is unclear due to the lack of accessible discernment. It's often hard to know one's path because you can't see it in a fixed moment. We use the metaphor of path because this journey is one of movement and travel, but at its root, the personal development process is one of unfolding.

A truth to which every parent is well accustomed is the often-imperceptible nature of growth. A child is growing by the moment, and through familiarity, we cannot see it, and then suddenly one day we look up, and our toddler is now in grade school and stands as tall as our waist.

The growth is so consistent and steady, like the water

which carves its way through the countryside and over millennia creates a great canyon, that progress cannot be observed in a moment. Much of personal growth and maturation follows the same process.

As a result, the "path" often is hard to see, so it is profitable to emphasize the vehicles used to move along the path instead of the path itself. What is the vehicle which will foster the continued blossoming into our final form? That's the sweet spot, and for many of us, that's Jiu Jitsu.

Carl Jung and Friedrich Nietzsche believed that one must become an apprentice before one can be free, that we must channel ourselves through a discipline, and through that necessary restriction we become something of value, which has more opportunities and capabilities for having been restricted and molded into something of utility.

The hallmark of a worthwhile vehicle is that it provides sustained Resistance in direct opposition to the path, like a ship always sailing against the headwind.

The vehicle takes you to where you want to go, but not so much through physical travel as through the opportunity of consistent Resistance which modulates the individual; it is the necessity of countless deaths and rebirths along the path that makes the vehicle both practical and beneficial.

DEATH AND REBIRTH

The death and rebirth motif is a hallmark of religious narrative for good reason: it is the proper behavior pattern of the hero. The hero is someone who voluntarily burns off the dead wood of his being, letting go of the attributes and habits which do not serve the highest goal, in the accumulation of characteristics better suited to the task at hand. The hero is the one who accepts the necessity of death on the way to the construction of his or her highest self, through the willingness to err, fail, and come up short on the way to the achievement of the ideal.

The path of progress is found through the cyclical wheel of aim, struggle, fail, incorporate the lesson, grow, and now aim higher and repeat. The individual with a fixed identity is half-dead; the path of life is to experience as many deaths and rebirths as your highest self requires.

This is Jung's idea of circumambulation, the journey toward the self, in which you experience as many transformations as are required to reach your self. Along the way, like a snake shedding its skin, you must let go of your former self to step into the next version of yourself. This is profitably considered a death and rebirth.

The hero's path is to voluntarily seek out these deaths and rebirths, with courage and conviction, to continue that inward expansion on the way to what we are destined to be.

Just as in the nature of caloric consumption, there is no life without death. The same is true for the psyche. The individual who remains stagnant is separate from life. The refusal of the call to adventure is the acceptance of the sentence of desperation. Life is a one-way street paved with Resistance, and the way forward is through the voluntary modeling of the phoenix: consuming oneself in flames to be born anew, better than one once was.

HOW MANY TIMES MUST ONE DIE AND BE REBORN?

There seems to be a predetermined number of deaths and rebirths required for each of us to attain the self. That number is different for all of us. For some we have several deaths and rebirths; it feels almost endless. For others, we are born almost fully formed and aligned with the self: we know what we are meant to be and possess a clear path toward its attainment.

My mom always wanted to be a mom. Since she was a young adult, she knew that's what she was destined to be (and she became a fantastic one!). There were a few deaths and rebirths, and then she manifested her purpose; she achieved her highest goal, making the world a more beautiful place in the process. For some of us, we are not yet fully cooked! We need more time in the oven and will require what feels like countless deaths and rebirths to reach the final destination of the self.

None is better or worse; each is a unique path of individuation as we fulfill our purpose. Whatever the fates have bestowed upon you, that is what you are here to become.

DEATH AND REBIRTH: A CHANGE IN PERSPECTIVE

Perhaps the greatest death and rebirth is psychological, as we upgrade the software we use to confront reality. The quality of our life is the quality of our inner dialogue, and our inner home is the emotions we repeatedly entertain. The great shift, the one that separates all great men and women of history, is exceedingly simple and wise: the primary focus is not what can we get in this life, rather, it is what can we give. "The secret to living is giving," as Tony Robbins says. That shift, the turning outward rather than inward, and searching for one's inner salvation through contribution, frees the soul.

We opened this book with a foundational premise on the misguided quest for retirement, a goal of inaction, which is based on the belief that life is meant to give us things. Always asking of life our various requests, looking to an external benefactor to grant our wishes, we have the situation inverted.

The game of life is not to see what you can get; it's to see what you can give. The modern struggle for meaning stems from a lack of contribution and worthwhile engagement. The profitable question to answer is how can I serve, what gifts do I possess to add to this magical game.

The unconscious individual asks what can I get; the conscious one asks what can I give. This in many ways is the proper interpretation of the trickster archetype in mythology. There is a motif that the trickster is the precursor to the savior, rooted in the notion that the trickster is the personification of our unconscious, and that the savior is the manifestation of consciousness; stated more clearly, the journey from unconsciousness to consciousness is the evolution of the individual, and therefore collective, in which unconsciousness, in all its folly, must precede the development of consciousness, in all its efficacy.

If we wish to succeed, we must first fail.

Often, the unconsciousness creates dysfunction and chaos through ignorance, and the rectifying agent of order and stability which transcends the unknown is the savoir-like effect of consciousness, bringing light to the darkness.

This is what Einstein was referring to when he said the same level of thinking which got us into a problem will not be the same level of thinking which gets us out of it. There must be a psychological upgrade. There must be a death of the old to make way for the birth of the new. We must transcend the unconscious through consciousness.

The savior figure, in all his consciousness, is one that operates from a higher plane of awareness and looks upon the external world for how he can contribute, for what he can give, rather than for what he can take.

The saints and sages have paved the way for us. Carl Jung believed that what we were seeking was wholeness, a sense of completion, and that in our movement from unconsciousness to consciousness, we experience a wholeness of our psyche, our being, and in the process of becoming complete, we would inherently ask less of the world, as we would need less; we would then look outward, by turning inward, and asking ourselves what can we give to that world, as one can only give from abundance, the by-product of consciousness.

One's relationship to the world parallels one's relationship to one's own Being. The psychologically poor man chastises the world for not meeting the external needs which are manifestations of an internal lack which is the result of unconsciousness. As he wakes, as he becomes more – more whole, more centered, more aware, and therefore, more alive – he no longer looks to the world to fill him where he is empty; he is now full, and that fullness will flow outward into his surroundings. It will flow uninterrupted, as the conscious and alive being who has that deep sense of completion cannot help but serve, his love and libido flow out of him, his reservoir and capacity grows with time, so that he will always have more to give and will never run dry, as his consciousness connects him with the fuel source of life, deep within his own being, that is the endless flow of all creation manifest in this finite individual.

The great shift in the psychology of modern man from getting to giving is that which unlocks the proper relationship to Resistance, one that sees the difficulties of life as a gift rather than a curse. This perspective is the immune system of the soul, which affords the individual seemingly limitless strength of will and energy in the face of untold difficulty because the difficulty now possesses tremendous meaning which can only be found when the individual looks beyond himself toward the collective.

"You sought the heaviest burden – yet found yourself."

– Friedrich Nietzsche

IDENTITY AND RESISTANCE

Tony Robbins is a tremendous source of pragmatic tools to change one's experience of life. He has a maxim which is pertinent to this discussion:

The strongest force in the human personality is the need to be consistent with one's identity.

I believe it is this need, when properly understood, which can be the support system for the changes we wish to embody, specifically with our relationship to Resistance. At its root, the experience of inner conflict manifested as Resistance – the impediment to voluntary movement forward toward a goal that comes from some unseen place deep within – is the attempt to maintain one's identity.

Because, simply put: if you create the change you seek to make, confronting Resistance in the heroic manner and experiencing a death and rebirth, then the part of you which dies has fallen away, thus creating a change in identity. And your identity – your sense of self, the ego, the "I," does not do well with less. It seeks stability. It will sabotage your attempts forward out of self-preservation.

Evolution is a conservative mechanism. Our genes adapted to an environment of scarcity in which survival was the primary goal, made possible through a conservation of resources. We were either actively seeking resources or we were resting. With our basic survival needs met, our biology is often still trying to rest, to conserve the resources which our genes do not realize are now abundant. So we stagnate. We delay. We experience Resistance as an impediment to our goal because we have a conflicting deeper goal of preservation.

Thus, in order to create effective change and bypass this hard-wired circuitry of stability and maintenance, we require a shift in identity. Luckily for us, all the difficulties that come with the creation of a new identity can by bypassed, for we do not need to create anything new, we must simply rediscover something old.

RECONNECTING WITH OUR TRUE IDENTITY

Consider again the archetype of the hero: the one who voluntarily works for the betterment of being, who confronts the difficult challenge and through that process is transformed into something wiser, stronger, and better, who then returns to his or her people with this newfound experience of being and shares what he or she has become. This process of death and rebirth is very much an experience of a shift in identity. Behavior patterns and beliefs which originally served the initiate are left behind in the journey of personal transformation. Those aspects of the identity have died off.

This change in identity is constructed by two components:

1. The environment demanded this evolution, and
2. The hero was willing to sacrifice what one is for what one had to become in the pursuit of the goal.

This is where Jordan Peterson comes in. Are you on the side of who you are or on the side of who you could be? Do you identify with what you are or with your potential? *Or better still, do you identify as the thing which exists across the transformations?*

That's the pathway to a new life and to self-enhancement, and the surefire way to transcend one's current identity in the pursuit of a more profitable sense of self. This is the principle behind a growth mindset which is the source of tremendous transformation for countless human beings across disciplines. This is in the linchpin in befriending Resistance.

RESISTANCE: A SOURCE OF CONFIDENCE

Perhaps we should not define ourselves by what we are. Maybe we shouldn't even define ourselves by what we could be. Maybe our best bet is to derive a sense of self from the behavioral pattern who continually embraces transformation, who willingly lets go of that which does not serve him and continually upgrades his mode of being to become increasingly better suited to productively confront potential and manifest blessings out of its possibility.

We must identify as that which seeks Resistance.

I would consider this meta-identity the greatest source of self-confidence and strength for the individual engaged in elevating one's position in life. In every arena – whether personal, relational, professional, or financial – the being who defines his- or herself as the one who lets the insufficient die off and who seeks the Resistance which is the prerequisite for growth is perpetually in a state of productive confrontation with reality.

This is the pathway to success. This is the road to elevation. It is also the way to properly navigate Tony Robbins's maxim which, as far as I can tell, is a hard and fast rule of psychic life:

> *"The strongest force in the human personality is the need to be consistent with one's identity."*

If this is immutable, we had better adopt an identity which serves us. And I use my worlds purposefully. I say adopt, rather than construct, because you cannot construct what is already present. That foundational identity of the hero is at the root of our consciousness.

Consider this through a Darwinian lens. Only the fittest survive. This holds true just as much for the immaterial as the material; patterns of interpretation, identities, and ideas all are subject to this law.

The hero myth is the fundamental human story, the "fittest" inner narrative, demonstrated by its prevalence in all cultures across all times. This is the behavioral pattern which is the source of man's triumphant success against the primordial dragon of chaos. This is the "semi-conscious" identity we possess when we respond to difficulty productively.

Our inner monologue points at this indirectly. Consider that inner voice which pushes us on during difficult physical exercise: "You've got this. You're doing it. Keep going." And the countless variations of these trite words of encouragement which bubble up in consciousness amid physical discomfort.

Physical exercise is a case study for this, because it reveals something deeper: we are at our best in physical discomfort when our relationship is one of being a predator, rather than prey; of seeking rather than being sought. The weak man or woman sees the workout as an outside force happening to them. The strong, the one who embodies the predatorial role, is the one who is voluntarily seeking the discomfort and moving toward it; the one who sees the Resistance as a gift to be received rather than a burden to be survived.

This is the manifestation of an identity which voluntarily pursues worthwhile struggle, because inherent within that is the recognition that the struggle produces favorable adaptation.

Our working model is that the strongest force in the human personality is the need to be consistent with one's identity. To work with the laws of the psyche, rather than against them, we must return to our deepest sense of self which has allowed man to conquer the nature world and keep chaos at bay: the one who voluntarily seeks out struggle on behalf of the better.

This identity is our birthright. It lies dormant in our genes. We must "awaken the ancestors" and return to that relationship with experience in which we are the hunter, not the hunted. It's an entirely different response both psychologically and physiologically.

It is this identity which completely changes the experience of Resistance. Resistance no longer is something painful that happens to us which we desperately seek to avoid; Resistance is the pathway to our continued evolution and a source of tremendous Freedom.

BECOMING: CIRCUMAMBULATION EXPLAINED

Carl Jung recognized an aspect of personal evolution which he called "Circumambulation." Likened to the motion of water flowing down a drain, which starts in a large circuitous motion and gradually shrinks in circumference until it reaches the sink, this describes the pathway of becoming.

We embark on a journey toward a goal, and upon reaching that destination, we experience two primary changes: we now are at a new vantage point, which means our perspective has shifted and we see more clearly; and second, that we have changed due to the nature of the travel and now possess better eyes to see. With this new perspective and vision, we adjust our sights on a new goal which is more closely aligned with our depths and continue our journey. We then reach that next destination, and continue on this trajectory toward the self, with each new vantage point bringing us closer and closer to our final form.

Just as the water's circular path toward the drain becomes smaller with each loop, so does the path from point to point of our inner evolution gradually become shorter, and the differences between forms increasingly less dramatic, as we funnel in toward what we are destined to become.

Each redirection toward the destination, and each revolution around the drain, each represents a death and rebirth.

It is profitable to demonstrate this inner development through the example of outward travel (which is proper, as one cannot advance inward without also advancing outward). When a distant destination is set as a goal and then attained, we as aiming creatures must set our sights on new heights and begin a new journey. Through each successive journey, we learn to leave behind the things which do not serve us on the path and will not serve us at that new destination.

This is addition by subtraction, as half the journey of personal development is to effectively let go of that which no longer serves you on your unique path toward individuation. These may be relationships, habits, inner narratives, or psychological tendencies. Whatever will not serve the highest good must be left behind.

Each personal transformation is a letting go of that which does not serve the highest goal and an acquisition of that which does. Slowly but surely, movement down the path toward our final destination affords us seemingly infinite opportunities to let go of the lesser and adopt the greater; to fashion ourselves, and the way we interact with the world, into someone who achieves that final goal.

RESISTANCE REVISITED

When one looks to the world through the lens of contribution, in an attempt to give rather than get, this updated psychology possesses a hidden jewel: an indefatigable spirit with an endless capacity for forward motion.

This strength, and all of its products in the external world, all will be manifestations of an inner knowing, which creates a unique relationship to Resistance.

In the final analysis, the only thing we really can offer another is who we ourselves become. The work we do on ourselves is our greatest contribution to humanity, for we are both a part of humanity and its servant; we bring ourselves into every encounter with another, and what we are radiates outward toward those in our sphere of influence (a sphere which grows in proportion to our inner development).

The shift from seeing the world as a forum for getting (meeting one's own needs) to giving (meeting the needs of others), from "I" to "we," changes the landscape of the world itself. The most meaningful and substantial change is our relationship to Resistance.

The shift toward giving is truly a shift toward becoming, for one only can give what one is, and when the primary goal becomes one of contribution, the tacit goal is one of continued development so one has ever more to contribute. This shift is the greatest contributing factor to the strength of the individual because this is what changes one's relationship to experience itself.

If the game is to give, the game by default is to grow. And growth only can be experienced out of necessity. The law of evolution is conservation. Only that which is useful maintains; the superfluous burns off.

Evolution is an interplay, a dance, between the organism and the environment. It is the environment which forces the individual to adapt and grow. The gym is the perfect metaphor for this: when we want to put on muscle, we voluntarily confront Resistance; that Resistance forces our muscles to expand to survive and thrive under that heavy load. Now having grown, we can handle more Resistance, so we up the weight and repeat this growth cycle.

Expansion of the psyche follows the same process. The Resistance that is an inseparable part of life (the Resistance from which we all had hoped to someday retire) is the catalyst for your development. When the goal is contribution, the goal is to grow so we have more to give, thus turning the Resistance of life which once was viewed as a burden as a gift; the Resistance is meant to serve our continued evolution so that we become more and have more to give.

Now life's difficulty is no longer suffering. Suffering comes from a feeling of hopelessness and clinging to untruths; suffering is a rejection of reality. But now we no longer reject. We don't even accept. We have transcended to appreciation.

All of life's Resistance becomes a gift because it is offering us exactly what we need: the environment which demands our growth so that we become more, and now having become more, have more to give.

This is why the savior figure bears the cross; it is the Resistance that we are willing to shoulder which is our contribution.

Entropy is the natural state of things, decay is always waiting at the door. Entropy is the punishment for unconsciousness. It is the coming to the light of our own Being that shares our light with the world. We shoulder responsibility because it is our greatest gift; we come to understand that we are fashioned for service and are constructed into a useful tool of humanity, not despite, but through our struggle.

The path of life is the path of Resistance. This is the

wisdom of the old story of King Arthur and knights seated at the round table, when the holy grail appears before them. They decided to go off on a quest to discover the greatest treasure, and upon reaching the dark forest, they split up and each knight goes into the forest at the point that is darkest to him, where there is no way or path. Because as Joseph Campbell says:

"When you are one the path, you are on someone else's path. And the goal is to find your own pathway to bliss."

That pathway is one of becoming, which can only be made manifest through the great trials and struggles toward individuation. This is only possible by following your soul's unique path, which by definition cannot be the path of another, and therefore must be walked by one's self. But the walking is the forging. We make the path by walking, hence its difficulty. The tip of the spear always takes the most damage; but it is also that which creates the most change.

To once again reference Peterson, "The difficulty is the destiny." This is an irrefutable law of psychic life: through difficulty comes salvation, maturation, and the opportunity for tremendous purpose.

Voluntary exposure to that which is feared (read: resisted) is curative.

THE MOTIF OF STRUGGLE

The hero's journey, the fundamental narrative of the human experience, can be summarized as the following: the initiate confronts (whether voluntary or involuntary) tremendous Resistance (whether entropy, malevolence, ignorance or chaos) to achieve a goal (a treasure, a supernatural gift, safety) and shares that hard-won victory with his people back home (who made the sacrifice in his absence in exchange for the gift with which he would return from his travels).

All great heroes encountered great struggle, that which forged them into the hero. No one watches a movie in which everything starts out great, everything goes great, and everything ends great. There is no story there. There is no reality there.

The motif of struggle is the central teaching of these hero myths, and the great lesson is how the hero responds to Resistance in a way that is profitable for both him (or her) and his (or her) people.

This need to descend before one ascends, to do the labor in the fields before the harvest, is a common motif expressed in all hero stories, and is extensively described in the works of Jung, Peterson, and Campbell. This is the core teaching in the process of becoming. To become, one must struggle.

This central teaching is communicated again and again:

"You sought the heaviest burden – yet found yourself."
– Friedrich Nietzsche

"In filth it will be found."
– Alchemical dictum

"In the cave you fear to enter holds the treasure that you seek."
– Joseph Campbell

"The difficulty is the destiny."
– Jordan Peterson

"He (the trickster) stands at the very beginning of the way to individuation."
– Carl Jung

Which one speaks most to you? Or have you found a similar adage which you have clung to during difficult times?

The central theme is that the path of progress, the way to becoming what one can be, must be found through the encounter with Resistance, the inevitable pathway to life. Each of these aphorisms represents a constituent element of the human experience which must be properly communicated if it is to be consciously integrated: the experiences of life are the grist for the mill of our Becoming.

FREEDOM THROUGH RESISTANCE

The soul ultimately yearns for self-fulfillment and expression, what Carl Jung termed "individuation." For those individuals with a strong libido or will, we see a ceaseless effort for self-manifestation. Something inside us strives to evolve, to make our material form and life-circumstance an outward reflection of an inner dimension and wholeness. The need to exert oneself not so much against, but with life, is a hallmark of the individuation process. We all seek the freedom to manifest ourselves, and therefore our intentions, within the world around us. Carl Jung said, "The gift of a lifetime is to become what you are." But how does one achieve such freedom in a world of seemingly limitless restraint?

Freedom is to be found in the voluntary confrontation with Resistance. In fact, freedom only can be found as the by-product of a marriage with Resistance.

In *Beyond Order*, Jordan Peterson describes creativity as a condition of limitation, saying it is the restrictions which are the prerequisite condition for creativity. That's why the genie, the granter of wishes, is packaged so tightly in the bottle. Genie, Genius, must be confined and restricted to have the necessity to produce something which transcends that restriction.

You are such a genie, and your bottle is your Resistance. The Resistance you encounter in the achievement of your goal is the necessary condition which will make manifest your continued evolution into the highest version of yourself; Resistance is the source of your greatest Freedom, to become what only you can be.

Jocko, Peterson, Nietzsche, Jung, and all the great myths have sought to convey this fundamental aspect of the human experience. Jocko tells us that "Discipline = Freedom." Jung and Nietzsche tell us to be an apprentice, to voluntarily subordinate ourselves to a discipline so that we come out the other end fully formed, and having manifested our potential into a capable being, we now have more potential pathways in the world. Jung tells us that we must descend before we ascend, embodying the archetype of the trickster before we become the savior. Campbell tells us that all the great myths say the cave we fear to enter holds the treasure that we seek.

What each great thinker says is that the way to freedom, to the manifestation of what we inherently are and could be, is through befriending the Resistance in direct alignment to our goal, which is the only pathway to our goal.

This is the dragon-gold motif which I wrote about in "Hero." The dragon and the gold are inseparable aspects of experience. The only way the gold (Freedom) is experienced is through the dragon (Resistance).

The dragon is the restriction which makes the gold possible, the lamp which houses the genie. The only way to your highest goal is the integration of the experience of confronting the gift of Resistance, the precursor to your salvation.

SALVATION THROUGH STRUGGLE

"Everything can be taken from a man but one thing: the last of the human Freedoms — to choose one's attitude in any given set of circumstances, to choose one's own way."

– Viktor Frankl

As far as I can tell, the last of all human freedoms, and the source of your truest freedom, is to welcome Resistance into your life and embrace it as the gift that it is. When you achieve this relationship to Resistance, you have achieved ultimate freedom. You become spiritually bulletproof, because now you have integrated the understanding which spiritual teachers have been communicating through the ages, which only recently has become discernable to the layman beyond the walls of the ashram.

As Ram Dass taught, everything becomes grist for the mill of your awakening. All our experiences, even the bad ones (especially the bad ones), become gifts along the path which further our progress as a developing being. This completely reframes the experience of Resistance.

Resistance is now happening for us, not to us.

The work of keeping your soul alive during modern living is to become a master of reframing, looking at life through a new lens to reinterpret your experience. The ability to digest an event and come to a deeper understanding of how it serves you, below the surface-level pain and discomfort, is to become a master at working with Resistance. I use my words purposefully, because you are not working against Resistance. Resistance is your collaborator in transforming you into what you are destined to become. You are co-conspirators!

Carl Jung had this idea to beware of wisdom you didn't earn. For our purposes, it does you little good to read through this text, understand it, and regurgitate this concept without deep reflection. The path to earning this wisdom is to apply the concept directly to your life.

Consider your darkest days, the traumas and conflicts, whether through malevolence or tragedy, that caused tremendous pain. Ask yourself: how did this experience serve me? What strengths did I develop as a result? How did this pain lead to a blessing in my life?

Truly seek to answer these questions, considering the aphorism that life happens for us, and not to us, and act as if it were true. Tony Robbins is right, the quality of our life is the quality of our questions. If you seek to genuinely understand why your worst days were your best days, you have achieved a level of freedom that few have and will have developed a proper relationship to Resistance.

Because when you become grateful for the Resistance of the past, you now have the opportunity to be grateful for your Resistance in the present. It is this gratitude which is the antidote to suffering. You will still ask "Why me?" in the face of difficulty, but out of gratitude, not martyrdom.

"Why am I so lucky to encounter such massive Resistance that will give me the opportunity to become what I am meant to be!? Why have I been granted such a gift?"

I am speaking from experience. My worst days, through this lens, are now understood to be my best days. Government shutdowns which almost killed my business. Tearing both pecs, being in slings for 4 months, and recovering from nearly endless surgeries. Awful mistakes in meaningful relationships. All of these serve as the foundation for the benefits I now enjoy.

Here's the test, provided by a simple equation. You'll

know you "earned" your wisdom to the degree of the severity of the original pain and the degree of gratitude you now possess for the experience. The more painful it was, and the more clearly you now can see its benefit, the more wisdom you have earned from the experience. And in this context, that wisdom is synonymous with freedom.

JIU JITSU AND RESISTANCE

The ability to pursue Resistance is a skill. Like all skills, this must be consistently trained, or it will perish. I have come to believe that the greatest benefit Jiu Jitsu provides us is the opportunity for endless encounters with Resistance.

Professor teaches a new technique that you've never seen before, and you are completely lost. Resistance. You do a hard round with a peer in which you are lovingly trying to kill each other. Resistance. You are partnered with a new white belt, and while you want to aid their development, you still seek to place yourself in positions of weakness in which they can challenge you. Resistance. Not to mention the Resistance you conquered when that quiet voice in your head suggested you take the night off and catch up on that Netflix show you've been watching.

Jiu Jitsu is an unrivaled vehicle for personal development because of the difficulty of the practice which trains this pattern of action. This process of voluntarily pursuing difficult things in pursuit of a goal is that which causes our growth on the mat to transcend into the rest of our lives.

If you are training Jiu Jitsu with conscious intent, the rest of your life will improve. As we learn how to ascend the hierarchy of Jiu Jitsu competence, we train the behavior pattern which makes the ascension of all hierarchies (and competence) possible, inevitably leading to professional and personal success.

But deeper still, the great benefit in consistently pursuing difficult things on behalf of progress is that now you know you are capable of such action. You begin to identify as someone who voluntarily confronts Resistance in the name of growth. This embodiment of courage becomes the default way you interact with the world, and through this paradigm shift, you have become stronger and the world less daunting.

Jiu Jitsu is the basic training for befriending Resistance. Jiu Jitsu is the environment which crafts you into someone capable of such productive action. Jiu Jitsu is the vehicle we use to achieve our highest self. The chokes, the takedowns, and all the fun Instagram techniques are all fodder for this experience. The true aim of martial arts is to live like a martial artist, to courageously live a life of honor, passion, and discipline. Jiu Jitsu teaches us to become martial artists through the art of properly navigating Resistance. This is the highest benefit. This is what transcends into the rest of our lives. This is how we become what we could be.

We use the gentle art to become hardened in the face of Resistance. The cliché, "We aren't learning how to fight, we are learning how to live," is not a sufficient explanation for the miracle we are experiencing on the mat. It's more accurate to say we are learning how to fight on behalf of our soul so that we can live.

We do this through the voluntary pursuit of Resistance. We train this skill on the mat so we can live this way in the world.

RUN THE PROGRAM

I wear contact lenses. Each day upon waking, my first task is to put in my lenses to give me the ability to see so I can properly navigate my day. Consider this relationship to Resistance your newest pair of contact lenses.

Each day upon awaking, put on this lens which allows you to see Resistance as a gift along your path. This framework on Resistance is a software, newly downloaded. You must daily run the program.

There will be no shortage of Resistance in your day. When you go to the fridge for your breakfast and are met with the option for healthy and unhealthy foods, that's Resistance. You get to the office and are presented with a difficult task on a tight deadline: Resistance. And that hard training session to cap off a long day, yep, Resistance.

While wearing this lens, you now can see Resistance more clearly. You deeply understand its benefit. Through this wisdom, you will rise to the challenge of the day.

This inner strength requires perpetual training. Just like I put my contacts in each morning, every day you must remind yourself of the role Resistance plays in your life. This can be done through mantras, journaling, inner monologue, or environmental cues.

Find a system that works for you. Keep running this program. Eventually it will become your default setting, and as it does, enjoy the magic that unfolds.

CALL TO ACTION

"Knowledge must be converted to action or it's worthless."

– Tony Robbins

The reading is coming to a close. Now it's time to live (and train). You have the capacity to confront life's challenges in the most productive way, because it's not confrontation, it's cooperation. Life continually is presenting you with the opportunities and challenges that will provide you the gift of growing in the exact way your development most requires.

Your Resistance is your curriculum. All that's left to do is to welcome it into your life, and where it is not found, go seek it out. You are meant to grow. You are meant to grow so that you have more to give. Contribution - that is the great source of meaning in this finite life.

That meaning is found through the adoption of

responsibility. This is the laborious approach to life. Put on your work boots, grab your thermos, and get to work.

The work is to meet Resistance head on with gratitude. The more Resistance you can encounter, and to the degree that it directly opposes the movement toward which you most need to go, the greater your life will become. There is no guarantee of success. Tragedy and malevolence find us all. The snake always finds its way into the garden. But this is your best pathway through life.

Pick your head up, move in the direction of the difficult, and do so on behalf of yourself and the people you love. When you do, everyone prospers. The only gift we really can give anyone is who we ourselves become. The individual must start with one's self if he or she is to create any lasting change in the world.

What you become is your gift to all of us and becoming is a one-way street through Resistance.

So I encourage you, with all my heart, to embrace the Resistance in your life. This is the natural state of affairs, there is no way around it. We just don't get gold without dragons. They are forever linked as two poles of the same experience.

Your Resistance is here to serve you. It is the elixir of life, the path which leads to your highest self. Pursue Resistance with the fervor you would your highest goal, because in the final analysis, Resistance is the highest goal.

POSTSCRIPT

You have no idea the potential influence you could have on your community. Please, devote your life to personal development. The most selfish act is the least selfish. By becoming all you could be, we will all prosper.

Your role in this world cannot be replaced. Your reach extends far beyond your grasp. The fate of the world depends on your pursuit of Resistance in the attainment of your highest self.

Devote yourself to the mission of manifesting what you could be. Please. We need what you have to offer.

Godspeed,
Chris Matakas

NEED A GUIDE?

WE WOULD NOT pursue mastery of Jiu Jitsu by ourselves. Why should life be any different?

Chris Matakas offers high-performance, psychology-based coaching for individuals and couples ready to embrace honesty and transparency and do the deep work of leveling up their lives. After creating a personalized curriculum, Chris serves as a detective on behalf of his clients' souls to help them uncover their deepest desires and plan a path toward living out those desires in pursuit of their highest self.

Coaching formats are available in both three-month retainer packages as well as rapid immersion experiences. Apply for high-performance coaching at:

chrismatakas.com/coaching

PRAISE FOR CHRIS'S COACHING

"Chris was a bright light to guide me out of one of the darkest times of my life. I went from being a good person to always trying to be the BEST version of myself that I can be."

—**Janet B.**

"My coaching with Chris helped me navigate through what could have been the most difficult season of my life, instead I see it as one of the most rewarding! Because of Chris, I now have so much clarity of purpose and a better understanding of my own internal drive."

—**Zach T.**

"Working with Chris has given me more clarity in my mission in life."

—**Tommy W.**

"Chris was my saving ferryman who guided me across a sea of desperation to a beautiful path towards the light. He is a beautiful soul. Because of Chris I went from being completely lost to being highly confident that I could handle the difficult problem that was presented to me."

—**Bill C.**

FURTHER LEARNING

LET'S KEEP LEARNING together! Join my newsletter to receive a free lesson each week in which I share the most important concept or idea I'm focusing on in my studies and coaching.

To join the Wednesday Wisdom email, go to <u>chrismatakas.com</u> and write your email address in the footer.

LEARN MORE

If you enjoyed this book and would like to read about using Jiu Jitsu as a vehicle for personal development, check out Chris's other books available on Amazon:

My Mastery: Learning to Live Through Jiu Jitsu

My Mastery: Continued Education Through Jiu Jitsu

The Tao of Jiu Jitsu

On Jiu Jitsu

12 Rules for Jiu Jitsu

5 Rules for White Belts

Hero: The Path Through Jiu Jitsu and Life

Jiu Jitsu Kids: Roman Redefines Winning

IMPROVE: Grow As If Your Life Depends On It

The Daily Martial Artist

On Behalf of Jiu Jitsu and Wholeness

CONNECT WITH US!

WWW.CHRISMATAKAS.COM

Explore
chrismatakas.com

Follow me at
@chrismatakasbjj

Email me at
chat@matakasbjj.com

Message me on Facebook
Chris Matakas or Matakas Jiu Jitsu

Text me at
(609) 952-6200

Join our email list at
chrismatakas.com

Printed in Great Britain
by Amazon